CONTENTS

WHY SMALL GROUPS?

In St Luke's account of the Early Church we hear that three thousand were baptised following Pentecost (Acts 2:41). Guided by the Holy Spirit, the newly baptised 'devoted themselves to the apostles' teaching and fellowship, to the breaking of bread and the prayers' (Acts 2:42). In a similar fashion thousands of people have found spiritual nourishment in faith-sharing, in reflecting on Scripture and prayer as part of a small group.

This resource feeds such small groups drawing on the Scriptures with each session clearly rooted in a passage from the Bible. As the Second Vatican Council Fathers emphasised 'in the sacred books the Father comes lovingly to meet his children and talks with them' (Dei Verbum, 21).

Fellowship is a vital part of small group participation. In these small groups you are able to get to know your fellow Christians better and to form strong, mutually supportive bonds. The living community is essentially Christian as Jesus 'did not come to save individuals without any bond between them' (Lumen Gentium, 9).

Members of small groups are encouraged to share and gain confidence in talking about their faith. It is this confidence building in a trusting environment that helps participants to 'love in all the circumstances of ordinary life' (Gaudium et Spes, 38). Our prayers together help us to become the dwelling places of the Holy Spirit that we are called to be (Sacrosanctum Concilium, 2).

HOW DO SMALL GROUPS WORK?

The sessions in this booklet are designed to last between 1 and 1 ½ hours. Those leading the session are, of course, free to add periods of silence, hymns and other readings of interest - these sessions are a guide but can be used as they are written.

It is vital that each person is given the opportunity to give their thoughts and share where they are on their faith journey. Small group sharing is not a place for argument or heated debate.

The atmosphere should be prayerful with the aim of helping each to feel welcome and conscious of God's loving presence. Soft music, candlelight, a religious image or crucifix to focus attention can all be used to help in this aim.

LIFT UP YOUR HEARTS

FOREWORD

My dear brothers and sisters,

This Jubilee Year of Mercy is for each one of us. Indeed, it is for anyone who desires to be deeply and lovingly accepted as they are and yet challenged and enticed to let God bring the best out of them.

St Faustina is celebrated for her devotion to Divine Mercy. In her diary she wrote: 'no soul that has called upon the Lord's mercy has ever been disappointed' (1541). It is with this reassurance that we approach the Year of Mercy; nobody should live with fear in their heart when there is this profound acceptance of God available to them.

As we consider the broken and wounded world in which we live, we can often see a marked lack in the quality and practice of mercy. The challenge for us all is to imitate Jesus Christ, the face of God's mercy, and to render incarnate the mercy and love we ourselves have received.

I am grateful for *Lift Up Your Hearts*, this booklet for the sharing of faith in groups, which will also be used widely for individual meditation. I am grateful particularly that it encourages us to consider the mystery and beauty of God's mercy together with the reality of our lives marked, so often, by sin. We will all have experienced, within our closest relationships, times of entanglement and brokenness, and the desire to start again. This is very much the pattern of the unfolding of God's mercy.

This season of faith-sharing is a chance to understand God's mercy afresh and experience its life-giving power. During this Year of Mercy we will come to see how God's mercy is the unfolding of his justice, not the replacing of it.

May the Holy Spirit sustain us and guide us as we contemplate Christ, the face of mercy, and the salvation he has won for us. Kyrie Eleison! Lord, have mercy!

Yours devotedly,

+ Vincent Nichols

Cardinal Vincent Nichols
Archbishop of Westminster

SOME FURTHER READING

Catechism of the Catholic Church (1992) (abbreviation: CCC)
YOUCAT (2014)
Pope John Paul II: Redemptor Hominis (Redeemer of Man), 1979 (RH)
Pope John Paul II: Dives in Misericordia (Rich in Mercy), 1980 (DM)
Pope Francis: Misericordiae Vultus (Jesus Christ, the Face of Mercy), 2015 (MV)
Pope Francis (2014) The Church of Mercy: A Message of Hope for All People, DLT
Raniero Cantalamessa (2015) The Gaze of Mercy, The Word Among Us Press
Scott Hahn (2003) Lord Have Mercy: The Healing Power of Confession, DLT
Mark P. Shea (2015) Mercy Works, CTS
Fr Ivano Millico (2015) The Door of Mercy, CTS

MAKING CONNECTIONS

Love Divine
(autumn 2015)
on the graces we
receive from the
Father through
Jesus Christ in the
power of the Spirit.

Sparks of Light
(Lent 2012) on the
universal call to
holiness and living
a life of Christian
virtue filled with
the grace of God.

Amazing Grace
(Lent 2013) on
the sacrament
of reconciliation
and the call
to continuing
conversion.

Jesus, My Lord
(autumn 2014) on
discipleship and the
conscious decision
to follow Jesus.

Other related books include:
Living as One on the Church and
Hail Mary, Full of Grace on Mary, Mother of God

LIFT UP YOUR HEARTS

ABOUT THIS BOOK

'Mercy has become living and visible in Jesus of Nazareth, reaching its culmination in him... In the "fullness of time" (Galatians 4:4), when everything had been arranged according to his plan of salvation, [God the Father] sent his only Son into the world, born of the Virgin Mary, to reveal his love for us in a definitive way... Jesus of Nazareth, by his words, his actions, and his entire person reveals the mercy of God. (*Misericordiae Vultus*, 1). *Misericordiae Vultus is Latin for The Face of Mercy.*

Lift Up Your Hearts, a faith-sharing resource for small communities seeks to encourage reflection on the mercy we receive from God, shown in Jesus Christ, the Face of Mercy, and how we are called to live a life of love and mercy ourselves.

It is divided into six group sessions each containing Scripture, reflections and prayers. Also featured in the booklet is a selection of images which may stir a thought or feeling in a way that the text could not. We also invite you to make use of simplified daily prayers drawn from the Divine Office (pp.54-61).

Lift Up Your Hearts is not tied to a particular time of year and the prayers and meditations may be used by individuals, groups or in a wider parish context throughout the year. This booklet and others in the exploring faith series can be viewed at and downloaded from the Diocese of Westminster's website [http:// rcdow.org.uk/faith/small-groups/resources/]. Leaders and members can subscribe to weekly bulletins during the season via **http://eepurl.com/ULaLr**

CHILDREN'S PAGES

Lift Up Your Hearts features pages specifically written for parents and grandparents to share the theme with children - featuring Theo, our young guide, pictured above. These pages contain a short reflection, a Scripture passage (from the Good News translation of the Bible), a question on the Scripture and some form of activity.

Image: Crucifixion with Dominican Friar by Oberrheinischer Meister (c.1400)

SESSION ONE **LIFT** UP **YOUR** HEARTS

THE OFFER OF SALVATION

THEME

> God is love and it is his profound desire to be merciful, to forgive us of our sins and deliver us from all evil so that we may be with him for all eternity. Made possible by the sufferings of his Son, God's loving act is freely offered to all who wish to enter into a transforming relationship with him.

Opening prayer

Adapted from Psalm 57(56) - said all together or the group can divide in half and alternate.

All: In the name of the Father, and of the Son, and of the Holy Spirit. Amen.

A: Have mercy on me, God, have mercy
for in you my soul has taken refuge.
In the shadow of your wings I take refuge
till the storms of destruction pass by.

B: I call to you God the Most High,
to you who have always been my help.

A: O God, send your truth and your love.
O God, arise above the heavens;
may your glory shine on earth!

B: My heart is ready, O God, my heart is ready.
I will sing, I will sing your praise.

A: I will thank you, Lord, among the peoples,
among the nations I will praise you
for your love reaches to the heavens
and your truth to the skies.

All: Glory be to the Father, and to the Son and to the Holy Spirit. As it was in the beginning, is now, and ever shall be, world without end. Amen.

As we come together let us, either aloud or in the silence of our hearts, give thanks and praise to the Lord for all the things we have accomplished, the joys experienced, graces received and people met over the past week. Let us also remember all those in need of our prayers particularly the poor and the sick.

Introduction to the Scripture reading

Let us go forward in peace, our eyes upon heaven, the only one goal of our labours.

St Thérèse of Lisieux (1873-1897)

Praying the Scriptures Luke 23:32-43

Note: The story of the crucifixion is familiar to us all, although with slight variances from account to account. In the Gospel according to St Mark and St Matthew, the two thieves join the crowd in mocking Jesus. The account by Luke, however, describes one as asking Jesus to 'remember him' when Jesus 'came into his kingdom'.

Two others also, who were criminals, were led away to be put to death with him. When they came to the place that is called The Skull, they crucified Jesus there with the criminals, one on his right and one on his left. Then Jesus said, 'Father, forgive them; for they do not know what they are doing.' And they cast lots to divide his clothing. And the people stood by, watching; but the leaders scoffed at him, saying, 'He saved others; let him save himself if he is the Messiah of God, his chosen one!' The soldiers also mocked him, coming up and offering him sour wine, and saying, 'If you are the King of the Jews, save yourself!' There was also an inscription over him, 'This is the King of the Jews.'

One of the criminals who were hanged there kept deriding him and saying, 'Are you not the Messiah? Save yourself and us!' But the other rebuked him, saying, 'Do you not fear God, since you are under the same sentence of condemnation? And we indeed have been condemned justly, for we are getting what we deserve for our deeds, but this man has done nothing wrong.' Then he said, 'Jesus, remember me when you come into your kingdom.' He replied, 'Truly I tell you, today you will be with me in Paradise.'

Please take a few moments in silence to reflect on the passage, then share a word or phrase that has struck you. Pause to think about what others have said then, after a second reading of the passage, you may wish to share a further thought.

Reflection

For elite level athletes, visualization is an integral part of their preparation for competition. They imagine the scene, even the sounds of the crowd, as they rehearse the perfect performance in such detail so as to sense how their muscles will feel at each step of their run, dive or jump. In a fashion, the great masters have visualized biblical stories before beginning their works of art and, in turn, through our senses, we are moved to meditate on their great works, to help us grow closer to the Lord.

Down through the ages, many great artists have tried to help us visualize the paschal mystery of Christ's suffering, crucifixion and resurrection. Their beautiful works of sacred art attract thousands to galleries around the world. Yet, these the pivotal moments in our Christian faith are actually made present in every celebration of Holy Mass. We often hear that the Mass is a special meal yet it is so much more. We are actually there at the crucifixion, at the foot of the Cross alongside his Blessed Mother, Mary and his beloved disciple, John to sense their unbearable grief and anguish as Christ was nailed to the cross (CCC, 618).

Most importantly, in the celebration of the Holy Eucharist, through our own bodies we can sense the unfathomable depths of his love. Christ shared his Father's loving desire to restore all of humanity to Himself. (*Love Divine*, Session 1) The depth of that love became visible through his greatest act of mercy: his incarnation and ultimate death on the Cross. Christ joined himself to humanity, to bear our sins though he himself was sinless. In love, he suffered and died for our redemption, to restore the offer of salvation to each one of us. As St John Paul II explained in his encyclical, *Dives In Misericordia*, 'The cross is like a touch of eternal love upon the most painful wounds of man's earthly existence' (DM, 8). This act of redemption involves the 'revelation of mercy in its fullness' (DM 7).

'Justice is also brought to bear upon death, which from the beginning of man's history had been allied to sin. Death has justice done to it at the price of the death of the one who was without sin and who alone was able-by means of his own death-to inflict death upon death. In this way the cross of Christ, on which the Son, consubstantial with the Father, renders full justice to God, is also a radical revelation of mercy, or rather of the love that goes against what

SALVE REGINA / HAIL, HOLY QUEEN

At the foot of the Cross, Mary, together with John, the disciple of love, witnessed the words of forgiveness spoken by Jesus. This supreme expression of mercy towards those who crucified him show us the point to which the mercy of God can reach. Mary attests that the mercy of the Son of God knows no bounds and extends to everyone, without exception. Let us address her in the words of the Salve Regina, a prayer ever ancient and ever new, so that she may never tire of turning her merciful eyes upon us, and make us worthy to contemplate the face of mercy, her Son Jesus. *Misericordiae Vultus, 24*

constitutes the very root of evil in the history of man: against sin and death' (DM, 8).

Just as during his ministry, he met with sinners, he meets us in our sinfulness. Even, at the moment of his death, he met the repentant thief. As our merciful God, he is there waiting for us in the tabernacle, not to give us what we deserve but to save us from what we deserve. He is there waiting to save us from ourselves; what we have done and what we have failed to do. What he gives is a gift, freely given, a gift beyond measure, the gift of himself – his love, his grace.

- Have we considered that, during Mass, we are at the foot of the Cross?
- How has the repentant thief modelled true repentance for each of us?
- Recognising his sinfulness, the repentant thief consciously asked for forgiveness. How are we able to do the same?

Closing Prayer – Salve Regina
You may wish to conclude with the Lord's Prayer, a blessing (e.g. p.11) or silence. A scheme of daily prayer, taken from the Divine Office, can be found on pages 54-61.

Hail, holy Queen, Mother of Mercy,
Hail, our life, our sweetness and our hope.
To thee do we cry,
Poor banished children of Eve;
To thee do we send up our sighs,
Mourning and weeping in this vale of tears.
Turn then, most gracious advocate,
Thine eyes of mercy toward us;
And after this our exile,
Show unto us the blessed fruit of thy womb, Jesus.
O clement, O loving, O sweet Virgin Mary.

℣ Pray for us, O holy Mother of God,
℟ that we may be made worthy of the promises of Christ, thy Son.

Almighty, everlasting God, who by the co-operation of the Holy Spirit didst prepare the body and soul of the glorious Virgin-Mother Mary to become a dwelling-place meet for thy Son: grant that as we rejoice in her commemoration; so by her fervent intercession we may be delivered from present evils and from everlasting death.

This session looks at the profundity of God's love for the world and of humankind. The desire of the Father to redeem our race and the obedience and love shown by Jesus Christ, his Son, culminate in the 'beauty' of the Cross. Next week we look more closely at the story of the Prodigal Son. In the meantime please make use of the 'journal' page opposite (p.11).

SIGNPOST

RESPONDING TO GOD'S MERCY WITH JOY

'The spirit of the Lord God is upon me, because the Lord has anointed me; he has sent me to bring good news to the oppressed, to bind up the broken-hearted, to proclaim liberty to the captives, and release to the prisoners; to proclaim the year of the Lord's favour.' (Isaiah 61:1-2).

Re-reading this session's Scripture passage (from the New Revised Standard Version) or perhaps from a different Scripture translation, you may wish to note a word or phrase that caught your attention, here or on your mobile phone, to refer to from time to time.

Holy Scripture is one way which our loving God communicates to each of us. What is your personal response, perhaps an action you might take, to the passage you have just read?

 Over the course of the next six weeks, consider making a note of something for which you are thankful on a scrap of paper. Place this in a jam jar or a small box and, at the end of the six weeks, empty out the slips of paper and reflect on the goodness, love and mercy that you have experienced and received.

The blessing from 2 Corinthians 13:14
May the grace of the Lord Jesus Christ and the love of God and the fellowship of the Holy Spirit be with [us] all. Amen.

1. JESUS' GREAT OFFERING

Hello, it's Theo, good to see you again. We've all got a bit older since we last met, my broken leg has healed and the cast has come off. Things change. There is one thing, though, that doesn't change - God's love for us. During the Christmas celebrations our parish priest reminded us that Jesus became a human baby out of love for everyone. On the Cross, Jesus died to save all the people of the world; even though he'd done nothing wrong.

From the Bible

Two other men, both of them criminals, were also led out to be put to death with Jesus. When they came to the place called "The Skull," they crucified Jesus there, and the two criminals, one on his right and the other on his left.

One of the criminals hanging there hurled insults at him: "Aren't you the Messiah? Save yourself and us!" The other one, however, rebuked him, saying, "Don't you fear God? You received the same sentence he did. Ours, however, is only right, because we are getting what we deserve for what we did; but he has done no wrong." And he said to Jesus, "Remember me, Jesus, when you come as King!"

Jesus said to him, "I promise you that today you will be in Paradise with me."

From the Good News according to St Luke, chapter 23 verses 32 to 43.

What did Jesus promise to the criminal who was sorry?
Have a look at the Bible passage above!

LIFT UP YOUR HEARTS

When Jesus was on the Cross, there were two others on crosses either side of him. One was rude to Jesus, the other realised who Jesus was and asked that Jesus remember him. The second one realised that Jesus was the Son of God and believed in him.

There are often times when it is difficult to do the right thing. Sometimes we can be so embarrassed that we don't ask for forgiveness. Jesus asks that, if we are sorry and want his healing, all we have to do is ask.

Can you find these words in the search box below?

Cross	Criminal
Jesus	Change
Sorry	Promise

Let us Pray
O God our Father,
help me to be like the criminal who said sorry. Help me to recognise the precious gift we have in Jesus your Son. Help me to show my love for you in the way that I live.
Amen.

C	A	G	L	E	F	Q	C	S	H
H	I	C	R	O	S	S	D	O	P
R	S	R	A	C	K	B	G	R	O
J	Y	I	Z	L	H	M	P	R	F
E	X	M	B	K	U	A	Q	Y	N
S	M	I	W	V	T	R	N	M	O
U	D	N	T	C	B	V	S	G	L
S	J	A	E	V	E	G	W	K	E
A	Y	L	I	F	H	J	I	N	J
D	Z	X	E	S	I	M	O	R	P

Image: Return of the Prodigal Son by Bartolomé Esteban Murillo (1667-70)

DISTANCE FROM THE FATHER'S EMBRACE
SESSION TWO

 The story of the lost son is a familiar one of selfishness, sin, repentance and forgiveness. Contrition, such as that shown by the son, is sorrow of the soul and detestation of the sin committed, together with a resolution not to sin again. Sin distances us from the Father; Jesus helps us to find our way home.

Opening Prayers
Taken from Psalm 51(50) – to be said all together or the group can divide in half and alternate.

All: In the name of the Father, and of the Son, and of the Holy Spirit. Amen.

A: You desire truth in the inward being;
       therefore teach me wisdom in my secret heart.

B: Create in me a clean heart, O God,
       and put a new and right spirit within me.

A: Restore to me the joy of your salvation,
       and sustain in me a willing spirit.

B: O Lord, open my lips,
       and my mouth will declare your praise.

A: The sacrifice acceptable to God is a broken spirit;
       a broken and contrite heart, O God, you will not despise.

All: Glory be to the Father, and to the Son and to the Holy Spirit. As it was in the beginning, is now, and ever shall be, world without end. Amen.

As we come together let us, either aloud or in the silence of our hearts, give thanks and praise to the Lord for all the things we have accomplished, the joys experienced, graces received and people met over the past week. Let us also remember all those in need of our prayers particularly the poor and the sick.

Introduction to Reading of Scripture
Let us listen carefully to the Word of the Lord,
and attend to it with the ear of our hearts.
Let us welcome it, and faithfully put it into practice.

St Benedict of Nursia (c.480–c.547) adapted

Praying the Scriptures Luke 15:11-24

Note: This passage of Scripture, the lost son, is part of a trio alongside the parable of the lost sheep and the parable of the lost coin which emphasise the Lord's joy at our repentance. Almost half of Luke's gospel account (Luke 9:51–19:27) is taken up with the journey from Galilee to Jerusalem. All the while, Jesus takes the opportunity to teach his disciples.

Then Jesus said, 'There was a man who had two sons. The younger of them said to his father, "Father, give me the share of the property that will belong to me." So he divided his property between them. A few days later the younger son gathered all he had and travelled to a distant country, and there he squandered his property in dissolute living. When he had spent everything, a severe famine took place throughout that country, and he began to be in need. So he went and hired himself out to one of the citizens of that country, who sent him to his fields to feed the pigs. He would gladly have filled himself with the pods that the pigs were eating; and no one gave him anything. But when he came to himself he said, "How many of my father's hired hands have bread enough and to spare, but here I am dying of hunger! I will get up and go to my father, and I will say to him, 'Father, I have sinned against heaven and before you; I am no longer worthy to be called your son; treat me like one of your hired hands.' " So he set off and went to his father. But while he was still far off, his father saw him and was filled with compassion; he ran and put his arms around him and kissed him. Then the son said to him, "Father, I have sinned against heaven and before you; I am no longer worthy to be called your son." But the father said to his slaves, "Quickly, bring out a robe—the best one—and put it on him; put a ring on his finger and sandals on his feet. And get the fatted calf and kill it, and let us eat and celebrate; for this son of mine was dead and is alive again; he was lost and is found!" And they began to celebrate.'

Please take a few moments in silence to reflect on the passage, then share a word or phrase that has struck you. Pause to think about what others have said then after a second reading of the passage you may wish to share a further thought.

Reflection

In an insignificant town, in a back street amid the animals, at the bleakest and coldest time of the year, Christ our light came into the world. The coming of the Messiah was expected to come with a blaze of glory, in prominence but instead came quietly, in isolation, in the darkest and meekest place. This unlikely entrance goes someway to helping us understand that God works in each and every place, in each and every heart, no matter the distance from what we believe to be the lightest and most grace-filled places.

There will have been times in each of our lives, no doubt, where darkness seems to pervade. There may even be times we have cause to ask ourselves whether or not we have been abandoned by God. We may have felt under tremendous pressure; in a time and place where all seems to be going wrong and each new thing seems a burden rather than a blessing. We know 'that the Lord our God is God, the faithful God, keeping his covenant of love with those who love him and keep his commandments' (Deuteronomy 7:9). What is certain, however, are those times where we have been the ones to abandon God.

The sense of isolation and dislocation experienced by the lost son is not hard to imagine. His was a separation entirely of his own making. He made his choice to leave the home he knew, the love he'd been shown, and follow his own whims and desires. This story has been likened to the cycle of sin and its cleansing through the Sacrament of Reconciliation. Lucien Deiss, a French liturgical musician, described this sacrament as 'the point where human misery meets divine mercy. It is the festival of God's tenderness. It is the discovery of the Lord who delights in showing mercy. Confession or Penance is rightly called the sacrament of mercy.'

There are 'many ways we can close ourselves off to the Holy Spirit; by selfishness, by neglect of what Jesus taught, living the Christian life in pursuit of personal interests' (*Pilgrimage Companion*, p.39). Denying Our Father's will, living in selfishness, is the equivalent of the son's self-imposed exile in the distant land. Like him we have a loving Father awaiting our return. Like him we very often find it difficult to recognise or even acknowledge our sins; yet the realisation of what we have lost - our life in God's loving embrace - should lead to a desire to go back, hoping in his mercy (CCC, 1432). Whatever our reasons for not returning – pride, a feeling that fault lies anywhere but ourselves – fear should never be an excuse.

SAINTS OF MERCY: THE HOLY CURÉ OF ARS

St John Vianney (8 May 1786 – 4 August 1859) was a French parish priest who became internationally renowned for his priestly and pastoral work in his parish and the radical spiritual transformation of the community. Of particular note was his persevering ministry in the Sacrament of Reconciliation - during the last ten years of his life, he spent 16 to 18 hours a day in the confessional. Even the bishop forbade him to attend the annual retreats of the diocesan clergy because of 'the souls awaiting him yonder'.

What is clear from this passage of Scripture is the arrangement anticipated by the son on his return. He was convinced that, owing to his actions, the most he could attain was the rank of servant (albeit a well-treated one). How true is this of ourselves? Seeking forgiveness, do we honestly consider the relationship which was damaged to be completely repaired? Indeed, when we offer forgiveness to others, can we honestly say that nothing is left of the brokenness? In this joyous passage, mercy is shown as a force that overcomes everything, filling a contrite heart with love and bringing consolation through pardon. Remember 'there will be more joy in heaven over one sinner who repents...' (Luke 15:7).

- Christ has willed that 'his whole Church should be the sign and instrument of the forgiveness and reconciliation that he acquired for us at the price of his blood' (CCC, 1442). When have we experienced the Church as such a sign?
- When did you last feel truly reconciled with God and with others?
- The heart is converted by gazing on Jesus (CCC,1432). What prepares our heart for repentance?

Closing Prayers – Westminster Diocesan Prayer for the Year of Mercy
You may wish to conclude with the Lord's Prayer, a blessing (e.g. page 11) or silence.

Father, slow to anger, abounding in mercy.
You see us and run to us when we are far away from you,
You find your way to us when we cannot find our way to you,
You are always faithful when we are unfaithful.

Jesus Christ, you entered the house of sinners,
You sat at the table of the poor,
You mounted the Cross, your throne of mercy.

Holy Spirit, you pour your healing gifts over our wounds,
You anoint us to bring good news to the poor,
You send us out as missionaries of mercy.

God of Mercies, have mercy on us,
so that where sin abounds your grace may abound all the more,
and we shall become like you, Merciful. Amen.

This session highlighted the lost son's return to his homeland with a contrite heart. Acknowledging our sins begins our own return and the grace of the Sacrament of Reconciliation. St Paul's encounter with the Risen Lord is next. A downloadable sheet on Reconciliation, to accompany this resource, can be obtained from **www.houseonrock.co.uk/mercy**

SIGNPOST

RESPONDING TO GOD'S MERCY WITH JOY

'The spirit of the Lord God is upon me, because the Lord has anointed me; he has sent me to bring good news to the oppressed, to bind up the broken-hearted, to proclaim liberty to the captives, and release to the prisoners; to proclaim the year of the Lord's favour.' (Isaiah 61:1-2).

Re-reading this session's Scripture passage (from the New Revised Standard Version) or perhaps from a different Scripture translation, you may wish to note a word or phrase that caught your attention, here or on your mobile phone, to refer to from time to time.

Holy Scripture is one way which our loving God communicates to each of us. What is your personal response, perhaps an action you might take, to the passage you have just read?

 Keep making a note of something for which you are thankful on a scrap of paper. Place this in a jam jar or a small box and, at the end of the six weeks, empty out the slips of paper and reflect on the goodness, love and mercy that you have experienced and received.

The blessing from Numbers 22:24-26
May the Lord bless you and keep you;
may the Lord make his face shine on you, and be gracious to you;
may the Lord uncover his face to you and give you peace. Amen.

2. JESUS SHOWS US THE WAY BACK TO GOD, OUR FATHER

I remember this one time when I got so annoyed with my mum and dad that I said that they didn't love me and I threatened to run away. I didn't mean it but I really felt it at the time. I know that they love me but sometimes, when I am asked to do things I'd rather not do, I demand to be left alone or say I want to go away and do my own thing. Jesus told a story about a Father and a Son, the Son wanted to go his own way and left home to do it.

From the Bible

Jesus said, "There was once a man who had two sons. The younger one said to him, 'Father, give me my share of the property now.' So the man divided his property between his two sons. The younger son sold his part and left home with the money. He went to a country far away, where he wasted his money, he spent everything he had. Then a severe famine spread over that country, and he was left without a thing. He wished he could fill himself with the food the pigs ate, but no one gave him anything to eat. At last he came to his senses and said, 'I will get up and go to my father and say, "Father, I have sinned against God and against you. I am no longer fit to be called your son; treat me as one of your hired workers." So he got up and started back to his father.

"He was still a long way from home when his father saw him; his heart was filled with pity, and he ran, threw his arms around his son, and kissed him. The father called to his servants. 'Hurry!' he said. 'Let us celebrate with a feast! For this son of mine was dead, but now he is alive; he was lost, but now he has been found.' And so the feasting began.

From the Good News according to St Luke, chapter 15 verses 1 to 12.

How do you think the Son and the Father felt in the Bible passage above - at the start and at the end of the story?

Jesus reminds us through this story he told that no matter how far we go away from God he waits for us to come home.

The younger son wanted everything his own way but soon realised that the best way to live a life was within his family. When he was away he realised that the Father treated everyone well and made sure they were well fed and happy. When he returned home he received a much better welcome than he had hoped and expected. Despite leaving home and turning his back on his Father - he got the best there was to offer when he said sorry.

Can you find these words in the search box above?

Father	Sons
Feast	Love
Pity	Party

Z	N	G	A	I	N	R	X	F	H
A	X	F	E	A	S	T	D	D	E
F	Q	A	L	Q	V	I	Z	W	H
M	F	T	F	J	L	O	V	E	D
L	N	H	M	B	O	K	C	G	E
Y	W	E	J	N	P	A	R	T	Y
Z	A	R	O	U	P	Q	Y	S	R
G	E	W	P	I	T	Y	V	N	E
N	B	P	T	R	X	K	S	O	U
X	C	F	H	S	M	B	T	S	P

Let us Pray
O God our Father, please help me to realise the times when I turn my back on you. Help me to return where I know I will be loved.
Amen.

Image: The Conversion of St Paul by Caravaggio (c.1600)

CONFRONTED BY GOD'S MERCY

SESSION THREE

THEME

A personal encounter with Jesus, the face of God's mercy, is transformative. Justified, that is redeemed by the power of the Cross, we are offered salvation. From the waters of baptism we emerge, like St Paul, a new person. Graced by Christ through the Spirit, we are empowered on our journey.

Opening prayer

Taken from Psalm 85(84) - to be said all together or the group can divide in half and alternate.

All: In the name of the Father, and of the Son, and of the Holy Spirit. Amen.

A: O Lord, you once favoured your land
and revived the fortunes of Jacob,
you forgave the guilt of your people
and covered all their sins.

B: You averted all your rage,
you calmed the heat of your anger.
Revive us now, God, our helper!
Put an end to your grievance against us.

All: Let us see, O Lord, your mercy
and give us your saving help.

All: Glory be to the Father, and to the Son and to the Holy Spirit. As it was in the beginning, is now, and ever shall be, world without end. Amen.

As we come together let us, either aloud or in the silence of our hearts, give thanks and praise to the Lord for all the things we have accomplished, the joys experienced, graces received and people met over the past week. Let us also remember all those in need of our prayers particularly the poor and the sick.

Introduction to Reading of Scripture

Let us speak of the God whom we love,
listen to the God who wishes to speak to us.
'Speak, Lord, for your servants are listening'.

Evangelii Gaudium, 146 and 1 Samuel 3:9

Praying the Scriptures Acts 9:3-21

Note: In chapter 8 of Acts, St Luke recounts the persecution undergone by the Church and the work of St Philip in spreading the good news to foreigners - a task Saul was to undertake after his conversion on the road to Damascus. Just as Jesus chose those with incurable diseases to show his healing touch, here he chooses and redeems the arch-persecutor.

Now as he was going along and approaching Damascus, suddenly a light from heaven flashed around him. He fell to the ground and heard a voice saying to him, 'Saul, Saul, why do you persecute me?' He asked, 'Who are you, Lord?' The reply came, 'I am Jesus, whom you are persecuting. But get up and enter the city, and you will be told what you are to do.' The men who were travelling with him stood speechless because they heard the voice but saw no one. Saul got up from the ground, and though his eyes were open, he could see nothing; so they led him by the hand and brought him into Damascus. For three days he was without sight, and neither ate nor drank.

Now there was a disciple in Damascus named Ananias. The Lord said to him in a vision, 'Ananias.' He answered, 'Here I am, Lord.' The Lord said to him, 'Get up and go to the street called Straight, and at the house of Judas look for a man of Tarsus named Saul. At this moment he is praying, and he has seen in a vision a man named Ananias come in and lay his hands on him so that he might regain his sight.' But Ananias answered, 'Lord, I have heard from many about this man, how much evil he has done to your saints in Jerusalem; and here he has authority from the chief priests to bind all who invoke your name.' But the Lord said to him, 'Go, for he is an instrument whom I have chosen to bring my name before Gentiles and kings and before the people of Israel; I myself will show him how much he must suffer for the sake of my name.' So Ananias went and entered the house. He laid his hands on Saul and said, 'Brother Saul, the Lord Jesus, who appeared to you on your way here, has sent me so that you may regain your sight and be filled with the Holy Spirit.' And immediately something like scales fell from his eyes, and his sight was restored. Then he got up and was baptized, and after taking some food, he regained his strength.

For several days he was with the disciples in Damascus, and immediately he began to proclaim Jesus in the synagogues, saying, 'He is the Son of God.' All who heard him were amazed and said, 'Is not this the man who made havoc in Jerusalem among those who invoked this name?'

Please take a few moments in silence to reflect on the passage, then share a word or phrase that has struck you. Pause to think about what others have said then after a second reading of the passage you may wish to share a further thought.

Reflection

Today, it is not beyond the reach of many to become a seasoned traveller. Short city breaks, country walking holidays and extended visits to different parts of the globe are not uncommon. With cheaper air fares and the opening of the Channel Tunnel people are much more able to travel to other countries. Most millennials have passports from before they can walk and think nothing of setting off to explore lands and cultures abroad. In a manner of speaking, we are changed through our life experiences including those that happen during our travels. Indeed, be it near or far, a lengthy journey or a few short steps, pilgrimage is an integral part of the Year of Mercy.

Some of us might have had life-changing experiences as Saul did in the Scripture passage we have just read. Saul was a committed Pharisee from Tarsus who, until that moment, had been travelling to Damascus to persecute Christians living there. Yet, rather than receiving what we might consider as justice - that is, what we think he rightly deserved for his fierce opposition to Christ's followers, he received justice 'to God's measure which springs completely from love, the love that flows from the Father and from the Son' (*Dives in Misericordia*, 7).

In the booklet entitled *A Pilgrimage Companion for The Year of Mercy*, Cardinal Nichols explains why an encounter with Jesus, the Face of the Father's Mercy, is so often transformative: 'Jesus took water from the Samaritan woman at the well; he touched lepers; he dined with tax collectors; he stopped the stoning of an adulterous woman. And in every case, he calls the person to conversion, to that change of life which is at the heart of God's mercy' (p.32).

We understand that, in his merciful love, God did not simply brush aside the sins of all. Instead, his beloved son, Jesus Christ, paid for our sins with the ultimate

SAINTS OF MERCY: ST DAMIEN OF MOLOKAI

Born Jozef De Veuster in Tremelo, Belgium, on 3 January 1840, he joined the Sacred Heart Fathers in 1860. In 1873, he went to the leper colony on Molokai, after volunteering for the assignment. Damien cared for lepers of all ages, but was particularly concerned about the children. He announced he was a leper in 1885 and continued to build hospitals, clinics, and churches, and some six hundred coffins. Damien, 'The Leper Priest', died on 15 April 1889.

FATHER DAMIEN OF MOLOKAI

sacrifice of his life - what St John Paul II calls 'a superabundance of justice' (DM, 7). Through his passion, death and resurrection, Christ restored for us the offer of salvation, which is often described as 'justification' (YOUCAT, 337). This restoration follows upon God's merciful initiative of offering forgiveness. Justification 'reconciles man with God. It frees from the enslavement to sin, and it heals' (CCC, 1990).

On that road to Damascus, our Lord reached out to Saul offering him 'mercy... a new chance to look at himself, convert, and believe' (*Misericordiae Vultus*, 21) and, in turn, with a contrite heart, the repentant Saul sought his forgiveness. Changing his name to Paul at the time of his conversion, Paul accepted God's offer of a share in the divine life, he was baptised and he began instruction in the Christian faith. In essence, he surrendered himself to the Lord. He was justified by the power of God's mercy!

Like Paul, with grace derived from the Holy Spirit's work of conversion, we too are justified at the time of our baptism, the sacrament of faith. Through the waters of baptism, we die to our old selves and emerge from the font as new creatures. 'We are detached from sin, which contradicts the love of God, and our hearts are purified' (CCC, 1990). It is by the power of God's loving mercy that we receive the grace to seek his will, in our free will, through our pilgrim journey.

- We read in the parable of the prodigal son and the encounter of St Paul the importance of a contrite heart. What is your experience of contrition?
- Do we consider the need for mercy and conversion to be ongoing?
- How might you explain the Sacrament of Baptism to a stranger?

Closing Prayers - Petition of St Nicholas of Flue
You may wish to conclude with the Lord's Prayer, a blessing (e.g. p.27) or silence.

My Lord and my God, take from me everything that distances me from you.
My Lord and my God, give me everything that brings me closer to you.
My Lord and my God, detach me from myself to give my all to you.

In this session, we have explored he experience of St Paul, who rose anew after his encounter with Jesus Christ. Ultimately, the offer of salvation is ours to fully accept or decline. Next session we will look at the parable of the Good Samaritan and our need of assistance and mercy. In the meantime please make use of the 'journal' page opposite (p.27).

SIGNPOST

RESPONDING TO GOD'S MERCY WITH JOY

'The spirit of the Lord God is upon me, because the Lord has anointed me; he has sent me to bring good news to the oppressed, to bind up the broken-hearted, to proclaim liberty to the captives, and release to the prisoners; to proclaim the year of the Lord's favour.' (Isaiah 61:1-2).

Re-reading this session's Scripture passage (from the New Revised Standard Version) or perhaps from a different Scripture translation, you may wish to note a word or phrase that caught your attention, here or on your mobile phone, to refer to from time to time.

Holy Scripture is one way which our loving God communicates to each of us. What is your personal response, perhaps an action you might take, to the passage you have just read?

 Keep making a note of something for which you are thankful on a scrap of paper. Place this in a jam jar or a small box and, at the end of the six weeks, empty out the slips of paper and reflect on the goodness, love and mercy that you have experienced and received.

The blessing from 2 Corinthians 13:14
May the grace of the Lord Jesus Christ and the love of God and the fellowship of the Holy Spirit be with [us] all. Amen.

3. BECOMING SOMEONE NEW

It is always interesting to hear where we come from. Whenever my mum and dad talk about the day I was born, it was freezing cold with snow everywhere, I sit up and listen with my eyes shut. The same is true when they talk about my baptism when they say that I was given a new birth!

From the Bible

As Saul was coming near the city of Damascus, suddenly a light from the sky flashed around him. He fell to the ground and heard a voice saying to him, "Saul, Saul! Why do you persecute me? I am Jesus, whom you persecute," the voice said. Saul got up from the ground and opened his eyes, but could not see a thing.

There was a believer in Damascus named Ananias. He had a vision, in which the Lord said to him, "Ananias! Go to Straight Street and ask for a man from Tarsus named Saul. Go, because I have chosen him to serve me, to make my name known." So Ananias went, entered the house where Saul was, and placed his hands on him. "Brother Saul, Jesus himself sent me, so that you might see again and be filled with the Holy Spirit."

At once something like fish scales fell from Saul's eyes, and he was able to see again. He stood up and was baptized.

From the Acts of the Apostles
chapter 9 verses 3 to 21.

What did the Lord say Saul had
been chosen to do?

Have a look at the Bible
passage above!

LIFT UP YOUR HEARTS

After Jesus had risen from the dead and gone back to the Father, Saul was one of the people who were looking to hurt and even kill the new friends of Jesus. In fact, he was one of the leaders of the group! Jesus knew all about this. He even said that when Saul was harming his friends, he was harming Jesus himself. Even though Saul was an enemy to Christians, Jesus called to him and Saul's heart was opened to Jesus' love. Saul was baptised and, from that moment on, he was one of Jesus' very best friends.

Can you find these words in the search box below?

Saul	Damascus
Baptism	Open
Spirit	Serve

X	Y	R	P	T	L	P	S	Z	T
S	U	C	S	A	M	A	D	B	I
A	C	A	E	N	F	G	H	J	R
U	K	Q	R	U	V	W	Q	V	I
L	E	L	V	V	E	N	T	W	P
O	O	N	E	F	I	F	T	E	S
E	N	T	W	E	L	V	E	A	Q
A	P	P	L	E	Q	N	E	P	O
X	P	T	I	A	M	C	O	O	L
B	A	P	T	I	S	M	H	A	T

Let us Pray
O God our Father,
speak to me and fill me
with your Spirit. Help me to say 'yes'
to your call. Amen.

Image: The Good Samaritan, after Delacroix by Vincent van Gogh (1890)

SEEKING A PLACE OF HEALING & SANCTUARY
SESSION FOUR

THEME

God responds to our weakness, pain and sin by reaching out to us in his infinite mercy. Moved with pity by our helplessness, the Lord acts with compassion to save us and restore us to full health as creatures made in the image and likeness of God.

Opening prayer
Taken from Psalm 23(22) – to be said all together or the group can divide in half and alternate.

All: In the name of the Father, and of the Son, and of the Holy Spirit. Amen.

A: The Lord is my shepherd, I shall not want.
He makes me lie down in green pastures;
he leads me beside still waters; he restores my soul.
He leads me in right paths for his name's sake.

B: Even though I walk through the darkest valley,
I fear no evil; for you are with me;
your rod and your staff – they comfort me.

A: You prepare a table before me
in the presence of my enemies;
you anoint my head with oil; my cup overflows.

B: Surely goodness and mercy shall follow me
all the days of my life,
and I shall dwell in the house of the Lord my whole life long.

All: Glory be to the Father, and to the Son and to the Holy Spirit. As it was in the beginning, is now, and ever shall be, world without end. Amen.

As we come together let us, either aloud or in the silence of our hearts, give thanks and praise to the Lord for all the things we have accomplished, the joys experienced, graces received and people met over the past week. Let us also remember all those in need of our prayers particularly the poor and the sick.

Introduction to Reading of Scripture
Let us go forward in peace, our eyes upon heaven, the only one goal of our labours.

St Thérèse of Lisieux (1873-1897)

Explore the Scriptures Luke 10:25-37

Note: Immediately prior to this passage we have the return of the seventy who were sent by Jesus 'as lambs among wolves' to share in his work. After the parable of the Good Samaritan, we read of Jesus continuing his journey up to Jerusalem, visiting the house of Mary and Martha, then praying 'in a certain place' where he gifted the 'Our Father' to the disciples.

Just then a lawyer stood up to test Jesus. 'Teacher', he said, 'what must I do to inherit eternal life?' He said to him, 'What is written in the law? What do you read there?' He answered, 'You shall love the Lord your God with all your heart, and with all your soul, and with all your strength, and with all your mind; and your neighbour as yourself.' And he said to him, 'You have given the right answer; do this, and you will live.'

But wanting to justify himself, he asked Jesus, 'And who is my neighbour?' Jesus replied, 'A man was going down from Jerusalem to Jericho, and fell into the hands of robbers, who stripped him, beat him, and went away, leaving him half dead. Now by chance a priest was going down that road; and when he saw him, he passed by on the other side. So likewise a Levite, when he came to the place and saw him, passed by on the other side. But a Samaritan while travelling came near him; and when he saw him, he was moved with pity. He went to him and bandaged his wounds, having poured oil and wine on them. Then he put him on his own animal, brought him to an inn, and took care of him. The next day he took out two denarii, gave them to the innkeeper, and said, "Take care of him; and when I come back, I will repay you whatever more you spend." Which of these three, do you think, was a neighbour to the man who fell into the hands of the robbers?' He said, 'The one who showed him mercy.' Jesus said to him, 'Go and do likewise.'

Please take a few moments in silence to reflect on the passage, then share a word or phrase that has struck you. Pause to think about what others have said then after a second reading of the passage you may wish to share a further thought.

Reflection
A story which made headlines in 2010 was the rescue of thirty-three Chilean miners trapped for over two months in a collapsed mine, almost half a mile underground. As the world watched, attempts to save them failed. Even the team of international specialists were left facing defeat. What remained was to pray. Incredibly, the drill broke through. A tiny capsule was then constructed to carry a rescuer down the narrow shaft to the miners. His task was to give them confidence to trust him and carry them one by one up through the darkness to safety - and to life! It was an emotional moment when all thirty-three had been brought back to

the surface; a disaster turned unexpectedly into the success story of the year.

Something similar happens in this parable. You might notice that the lawyer's real question is how 'to inherit eternal life'. When he gives the correct answer, it becomes obvious that it is an impossible thing for anyone to do alone. Because of our sinfulness, we cannot love God just as we are. We cannot love God perfectly. We need help. Like the Chilean miners unable to save themselves, it is even more impossible to free ourselves from sin and reach God by our efforts alone. We need The Rescuer; the one who willingly takes responsibility so as to restore us to light and life, who 'has rescued us from the power of darkness and transferred us into the kingdom of his beloved Son' (Colossians 1:13, cf. Psalm 107:19). As we read in the Catechism: 'The Gospel is the revelation in Jesus Christ of God's mercy to sinners' (cf. Matthew 1:21 and CCC, 1846).

The Fathers of the Church, notably Augustine, in the figure of the Good Samaritan recognised Christ coming to the rescue of humanity. Attacked by the devil, man lies 'half-dead', stripped of the supernatural life of grace and wounded by sin. The priest and Levite symbolise the Old Testament, unable to lift humankind up the infinite distance to God. The Good News is God's mercy which moves him to get involved in our mess in order to save and heal us. The oil and wine poured generously are the medicine of the Holy Spirit and of Christ's own Blood which restores our wounded nature. The Son of God takes responsibility for our sins and carries us to the inn, the Church, founded to look after us until he comes again (cf. CCC, 1421). Perhaps this is what Pope Francis means when he speaks of the Church as 'a field hospital'. (Homily, 2 February 2015).

And as St John Paul II wrote in his encyclical, *Dives in Misericordiae*: 'The

SAINTS OF MERCY: ST JOHN OF GOD

St John of God (8 March 1495 – 8 March 1550) was a Portuguese-born soldier, moved initially by a sermon of St John of Ávila, turned health-care worker in Spain. He established a house where he tended to the needs of the sick poor, begging to raise funds. One story recounts how he went into a burning hospital to save trapped patients - he is the patron saint of firefighters! His followers later formed the Brothers Hospitallers of St John of God, a worldwide religious institute dedicated to the care of the poor sick and those suffering from mental disorders.

Church lives an authentic life when she professes and proclaims mercy - the most stupendous attribute of the Creator and of the Redeemer - and when she brings people close to the sources of the Saviour's mercy... It is the Sacrament of Reconciliation that prepares the way for each individual, even those weighed down with great faults. In this sacrament each person can experience love which is more powerful than sin... It is precisely because sin exists in the world, which "God so loved...that he gave his only Son," that God, who "is love," cannot reveal Himself otherwise than as mercy' (DM,13).

The lawyer had not approached Jesus in friendship but to test him, as an adversary. Original sin is this, man's hostile mistrust of God. Yet, despite the times we do not fully trust in him, God remains our only hope of rescue. He does not treat us as we deserve but in his mercy saves us in spite of our frequent ingratitude. Likewise, it was the despised Samaritan who, having pity, showed mercy. Gospel mercy, as St Josemaría Escrivá says, means more than a compassionate attitude. It means 'keeping one's heart totally alive, throbbing in a way that is both human and divine, with a love that is strong, self-sacrificing and generous.' Christian compassion demands that we 'get involved' (*Evangelii Gaudium*, 24) not only with those we might distrust, but also those who mistrust us.

- How might our small group or parish community be a place of healing?
- What can you recall of the stories featuring Jesus' practice of mercy?
- How can we exhibit a heart 'totally alive', self-sacrifice and generosity?

Closing Prayers - derived from Psalm 84
You may wish to conclude with the Lord's Prayer, a blessing (e.g. p.35) or silence.

Almighty and ever-living God,
the God who loves each one of us.
We praise you with great joy,
we implore you with confidence and hope.
In you is all mercy and faithfulness,
in your heart justice and peace embrace;
May your faithfulness spring from the earth
and your justice look down from heaven.

This session looked at the parable of the Good Samaritan as a metaphor for the healing we, ourselves, receive from Christ through the Church. We also explored showing mercy as 'keeping our heart totally alive'. Next session, we will see the results of the encounter between Zacchaeus and Jesus. In the meantime please make use of the page opposite.

SIGNPOST

RESPONDING TO GOD'S MERCY WITH JOY

The spirit of the Lord God is upon me, because the Lord has anointed me; he has sent me to bring good news to the oppressed, to bind up the broken-hearted, to proclaim liberty to the captives, and release to the prisoners; to proclaim the year of the Lord's favour.' (Isaiah 61:1-2).

Re-reading this session's Scripture passage (from the New Revised Standard Version) or perhaps from a different Scripture translation, you may wish to note a word or phrase that caught your attention, here or on your mobile phone, to refer to from time to time.

Holy Scripture is one way which our loving God communicates to each of us. What is your personal response, perhaps an action you might take, to the passage you have just read?

 Keep making a note of something for which you are thankful on a scrap of paper. Place this in a jam jar or a small box and, at the end of the six weeks, empty out the slips of paper and reflect on the goodness, love and mercy that you have experienced and received.

The blessing from Numbers 22:24-26
May the Lord bless you and keep you;
may the Lord make his face shine on you, and be gracious to you;
may the Lord uncover his face to you and give you peace. Amen.

4. HELPED BY THE CHURCH

Occasionally there are fights in the playground, sometimes people call each other names and sometimes people hit one another. Of course, we know that we shouldn't hurt other people - our teachers and our parents always remind us about this. When someone is hurt then there is always a rush to help from their friends, others hang back watching what is happening and don't want to get involved. Jesus reminds us in the story of the Good Samaritan that when we help someone else, we are helping him.

From the Bible

Jesus said, "There was once a man who was going down from Jerusalem to Jericho when robbers attacked him, stripped him, and beat him up, leaving him half dead. It so happened that a priest was going down that road; but when he saw the man, he walked on by on the other side. In the same way a Levite also came there, went over and looked at the man, and then walked on by on the other side. But a Samaritan who was travelling that way came upon the man, and when he saw him, his heart was filled with pity. He went over to him, poured oil and wine on his wounds and bandaged them; then he put the man on his own animal and took him to an inn, where he took care of him.

From the Good News according to St Luke, chapter 10 verses 29 to 37.

Which one of the priest, the Levite or the Samaritan do you think Jesus said was a 'neighbour' to the wounded man?

Have a look at the Bible passage above!

There were probably very good reasons for the priest and the Levite not to help the man on the road to Jericho. The point that Jesus makes here is that help can often come from a strange and unexpected source.

The inn we read about in the story symbolises the Church. Jesus, himself, is the Good Samaritan who picks us up when we are battered and bruised and cares for us, healing our wounds with wine - his precious blood poured out for us. We know that he wants us to be happy and whole - we can help others when they are hurt and we can help them ask for Jesus to be there too.

Can you find these words in the search box above?

Journey	Jericho
Rescue	Mercy
Healing	Church

Q	J	O	U	R	N	E	Y	X	Z
Y	P	A	B	C	D	U	E	F	G
H	I	J	E	R	I	C	H	O	J
G	K	L	M	N	O	S	P	Q	R
N	S	T	U	V	W	E	X	Y	Z
I	R	I	C	H	U	R	C	H	E
L	A	L	Q	P	H	N	R	O	T
A	L	R	X	Z	Y	G	O	S	K
E	E	M	E	R	C	Y	I	P	O
H	N	Y	O	M	I	N	E	R	Z

Let us Pray

O God our Father, help me to see that when I help someone in need I am helping your Son, Jesus. Please give me the strength and courage to help others when it is easier to stand aside. Amen.

Image: Jesus Christ and Zacchaeus on a capital of Saint-Nectaire church (Puy-de-Dôme, France)

SESSION FIVE **LIFT UP YOUR** HEARTS

REPENTANCE AND TRANSFORMATION

SESSION FIVE

THEME

St Faustina wrote in her Diary that 'God cannot punish even the greatest sinner if he makes an appeal to His compassion' (1146). This session considers the appeal of Zacchaeus and the response he gave to a profound and life-giving encounter with the compassion and mercy of God, in Jesus Christ.

Opening prayer

Taken from Psalm 145(144) – to be said all together or the group can divide in half and alternate.

All: In the name of the Father, and of the Son, and of the Holy Spirit. Amen.

A: Every day I will bless you,
and praise your name for ever and ever.
Great is the Lord, and greatly to be praised;
his greatness is unsearchable.

B: One generation shall laud your works to another,
and shall declare your mighty acts.
On the glorious splendour of your majesty,
and on your wondrous works, I will meditate.

A: The Lord is gracious and merciful,
slow to anger and abounding in steadfast love.
The Lord is good to all,
and his compassion is over all that he has made

B: The Lord upholds all who are falling,
and raises up all who are bowed down.

A: The Lord is just in all his ways,
and kind in all his doings.

All: Glory be to the Father, and to the Son and to the Holy Spirit. As it was in the beginning, is now, and ever shall be, world without end. Amen.

As we come together let us, either aloud or in the silence of our hearts, give thanks and praise to the Lord for all the things we have accomplished, the joys experienced, graces received and people met over the past week. Let us also remember all those in need of our prayers particularly the poor and the sick.

Introduction to Reading of Scripture

Let us go forward in peace, our eyes upon heaven, the only one goal of our labours.

St Thérèse of Lisieux (1873-1897)

Praying the Scriptures Luke 19:1-10

Note: This passage of Scripture is immediately preceded by the healing of the man born blind. Zacchaeus, the likely hated Roman conspirator is called out by name to share food with Jesus. The conversion of heart experienced by Zacchaeus is followed by the parable of the talents warning those gathered in the crowds to make full use of what is entrusted to them. After this we see Jesus on the Mount of Olives anticipating his entry to Jerusalem.

Jesus entered Jericho and was passing through it. A man was there named Zacchaeus; he was a chief tax-collector and was rich. He was trying to see who Jesus was, but on account of the crowd he could not, because he was short in stature. So he ran ahead and climbed a sycamore tree to see him, because he was going to pass that way. When Jesus came to the place, he looked up and said to him, 'Zacchaeus, hurry and come down; for I must stay at your house today.' So he hurried down and was happy to welcome him. All who saw it began to grumble and said, 'He has gone to be the guest of one who is a sinner.' Zacchaeus stood there and said to the Lord, 'Look, half of my possessions, Lord, I will give to the poor; and if I have defrauded anyone of anything, I will pay back four times as much.' Then Jesus said to him, 'Today salvation has come to this house, because he too is a son of Abraham. For the Son of Man came to seek out and to save the lost.'

Please take a few moments in silence to reflect on the passage, then share a word or phrase that has struck you. Pause to think about what others have said then after a second reading of the passage you may wish to share a further thought.

Reflection

We all know that love stories usually start with an initial attraction; perhaps the classic eyes meeting in a mysterious recognition across a crowded space. There follows a time of making 'best impressions', to try and captivate the other with our talents, wit, charm. Inevitably there comes a moment of truth, because the only way love can blossom and grow is in accepting one another warts and all. So in the classic love story, that first mutual gaze eventually ends in a happily ever after of bride and groom emerging side by side from the church, ready to tackle together all that life has in store for them.

Zacchaeus finds Jesus irresistible. So much so that he doesn't stand on dignity but scrambles up a tree curious to see him. Yet at the same time there is safety in the tree. Hidden among the leaves, he can observe Jesus without being seen, keeping Jesus at arm's length, with no fear of coming into close contact. However, Jesus spots him and looks him straight in the eye. Zacchaeus must have gone through a whole cocktail of emotions! Imagine how we'd feel being spotted by the Pope or the Queen and then being told that they wanted to come round for supper. Hugely privileged, yes, but also quite a bit flustered! Did Zacchaeus feel an extra twinge of discomfort at the thought of Jesus entering his house and privacy, his lifestyle set up by corrupt tax-dealings? Yet the Lord enters and takes Zacchaeus as he finds him. But he does not leave him there.

Jesus is not 'making a statement' in sharing dinner with a sinner yet keeping his moral distance. Jesus' look not only penetrates Zacchaeus' innermost being, but also exposes His own divine and merciful tenderness. There is a genuine exchange of hearts. Looking at Truth in the eye, Zacchaeus sees his life as it truly is. This means repentance, a complete change of perspective, an about-turn of priorities, a willingness to 'make good' injustices committed, to having the same vision as the Lord. The Catechism calls this an interior conversion of the heart: 'a radical reorientation of our whole life, a return...to God with all our heart, an end of sin, a turning away from evil, with repugnance toward the evil actions we have committed. At the same time it entails the desire and resolution to change one's life, with hope in God's mercy and trust in the help of his grace' (CCC, 1432).

As St John Paul II wrote: 'Jesus Christ taught that we not only receive and experience the mercy of God, but that we are also called "to practise mercy" towards others: "Blessed are the merciful, for they shall obtain mercy." The

SAINTS OF MERCY: ST FAUSTINA KOWALSKA

Saint Faustina was born Helena Kowalska in a small village west of Lodz, Poland on 25 August 1905. In the 1930's, Sister Faustina received from the Lord a message of mercy to be spread throughout the world. She was asked to become the apostle of God's mercy, a model of how to be merciful to others, and an instrument for re-emphasizing God's plan of mercy for the world. Her entire life, in imitation of Christ's, was to be a sacrifice - a life lived for others. Her diary, *Divine Mercy in My Soul*, has become the handbook for devotion to the Divine Mercy.

Church sees in these words a call to action. All the beatitudes of the Sermon on the Mount indicate the way of conversion and of reform of life... Man attains to the merciful love of God, His mercy, to the extent that he himself is interiorly transformed in the spirit of that love towards his neighbour' (DM, 14).

Again from St John Paul II: 'In no passage of the Gospel message does forgiveness, or mercy as its source, mean indulgence towards evil, towards scandals, towards injury or insult. In any case, reparation for evil and scandal, compensation for injury, and satisfaction for insult are conditions for forgiveness' (DM,14). Zacchaeus confirmed his inner conversion with compensation and action. He made satisfaction for his fraudulent past showing true repentance, mercy and generosity of heart.

Jesus meets us where he finds us, but does not leave us there. In the Sacraments of Reconciliation and Holy Communion, the Saviour empties us of sin and feeds us himself so as to change our natural self-interest into Christian self-giving. We are told to sin no more (John 8:11) and to go in peace to love and serve the Lord. Mercy cannot help but flow from God to us then on to our neighbour, for mercy is the economy of the Kingdom. 'If we have received the love which restores meaning to our lives, how can we fail to share that love with others?' (EG,8).

- How eager are we to let Jesus transform our lives with his look?
- How might we avoid seeking to make a statement with our acts of mercy?
- Might we describe our relationship with Jesus as a 'love story'?

Closing Prayers - From the Diary of St Faustina (950)
You may wish to conclude with the Lord's Prayer, a blessing (e.g. p.43) or silence.

Eternal God,
in whom mercy is endless and the treasury of compassion inexhaustible,
look kindly upon us and increase Your mercy in us,
that in difficult moments
we might not despair nor become despondent,
but with great confidence submit ourselves to
Your holy will, which is Love and Mercy itself.

This session looked at the transformative encounter between Zacchaeus and Jesus - an encounter which caused a complete change in the small tax collector. Next session we will look at the need for us to mend our ways and make a positive and immediate effort to demonstrate mercy, to be merciful as the Father. In the meantime have a look at the page opposite.

SIGNPOST

RESPONDING TO GOD'S MERCY WITH JOY

The spirit of the Lord God is upon me, because the Lord has anointed me; he has sent me to bring good news to the oppressed, to bind up the broken-hearted, to proclaim liberty to the captives, and release to the prisoners; to proclaim the year of the Lord's favour.' (Isaiah 61:1-2).

Re-reading this session's Scripture passage (from the New Revised Standard Version) or perhaps from a different Scripture translation, you may wish to note a word or phrase that caught your attention, here or on your mobile phone, to refer to from time to time.

Holy Scripture is one way which our loving God communicates to each of us. What is your personal response, perhaps an action you might take, to the passage you have just read?

 Keep making a note of something for which you are thankful on a scrap of paper. Place this in a jam jar or a small box and, at the end of the six weeks, empty out the slips of paper and reflect on the goodness, love and mercy that you have experienced and received.

The blessing from 2 Corinthians 13:14
May the grace of the Lord Jesus Christ and the love of God and the fellowship of the Holy Spirit be with [us] all. Amen.

5. SAYING SORRY

There are times when someone famous visits the town and there is a great, big crowd looking to see our visitor. For someone of my age and height, unless you are right at the front, you can't see and need to sit on someone's shoulders. When Jesus came to Jericho a little man, called Zacchaeus, wanted to see him so he climbed up a tree. Zacchaeus' day got even better when Jesus, the famous visitor, asked to stay in his house for dinner.

From the Bible

Jesus went on into Jericho and was passing through. There was a chief tax collector there named Zacchaeus, who was rich. He was trying to see who Jesus was, but he was a little man and could not see Jesus because of the crowd. So he ran ahead of the crowd and climbed a sycamore tree to see Jesus, who was going to pass that way. When Jesus came to that place, he looked up and said to Zacchaeus, "Hurry down, Zacchaeus, because I must stay in your house today."All the people who saw it started grumbling, "This man has gone as a guest to the home of a sinner!" Zacchaeus stood up and said to the Lord, "Listen, sir! I will give half my belongings to the poor, and if I have cheated anyone, I will pay back four times as much."

From the Good News according to St Luke, chapter 19 verses 1 to 10.

What does Zacchaeus promise Jesus that he would do?

People like Zacchaeus were not very well liked - they took people's money and sometimes cheated people out of their possessions. However, Jesus knew the heart of this little man. He didn't follow the crowd in disliking Zacchaeus but ate with him and helped him to see what he had done wrong. Zacchaeus was really keen to act like a true follower of Jesus from then on.

Can you find these words in the search box below?

Forgive	Tree
Repay	Power
Return	Restore

Z	R	E	W	O	P	F	G	U	E
L	E	I	L	A	K	O	N	Y	D
M	R	R	C	B	H	R	S	J	B
Q	O	I	H	R	P	G	T	O	K
Y	T	R	E	E	Z	I	B	M	N
G	S	U	F	P	F	V	X	R	V
J	E	D	X	A	C	E	U	I	H
L	R	G	N	Y	J	T	N	W	S
E	C	P	R	T	E	F	A	V	Q
T	M	A	E	R	U	O	K	W	D

Let us Pray
O God our Father,
just as Zacchaeus met your Son and
his life was changed; please help us
to see what we can do to make the
world and ourselves better through
his help. Amen.

Image: The Parable of Lazarus by Fyodor Bronnikov (1886)

LOVE EXPERIENCED & LOVE RETURNED
SESSION SIX

In Jesus' cautionary parable of the Rich Man and Lazarus, he warns that we will be judged on the love we show others. This season of sharing and this Jubilee Year are opportunities to assess how we are transformed by the love we have been shown and seek to extend such mercy to others.

Opening prayer
Taken from Psalm 86(85) - to be said all together or the group can divide in half and alternate.

All: In the name of the Father, and of the Son, and of the Holy Spirit. Amen.

A: Turn your ear, O Lord, and give answer
for I am poor and needy.
You are my God, have mercy on me, Lord,
for I cry to you all the day long.

B: O Lord, you are good and forgiving,
full of love to all who call.
Give heed, O Lord, to my prayer.

B: Show me, Lord, your way
so that I may walk in your truth.
Guide my heart to fear your name.

All: God of mercy and compassion,
slow to anger, O Lord, abounding in love and truth,
turn and take pity on me.

All: Glory be to the Father, and to the Son and to the Holy Spirit. As it was in the beginning, is now, and ever shall be, world without end. Amen.

As we come together let us, either aloud or in the silence of our hearts, give thanks and praise to the Lord for all the things we have accomplished, the joys experienced, graces received and people met over the past week. Let us also remember all those in need of our prayers particularly the poor and the sick.

Introduction to Reading of Scripture
Christ be with me, Christ within me, Christ behind me, Christ before me, Christ beside me, Christ to win me, Christ to comfort me and restore me.

attributed to St Patrick (c.387 – 493 or c.460)

Praying the Scriptures Luke 16:19-31

Note: The parables that talk about life after death, as this one does, are not intended to terrify the listener. Instead, Jesus is interested in 'today' and brings the future in to play to challenge his contemporaries and us. Through the gospels, Jesus repeatedly draws comparisons between those exalted by man and those ignored and despised - God's ways, however, are not man's! Only Luke's gospel account compares the beatitudes with warnings (Luke 6:20-38).

'There was a rich man who was dressed in purple and fine linen and who feasted sumptuously every day. And at his gate lay a poor man named Lazarus, covered with sores, who longed to satisfy his hunger with what fell from the rich man's table; even the dogs would come and lick his sores. The poor man died and was carried away by the angels to be with Abraham. The rich man also died and was buried. In Hades, where he was being tormented, he looked up and saw Abraham far away with Lazarus by his side. He called out, "Father Abraham, have mercy on me, and send Lazarus to dip the tip of his finger in water and cool my tongue; for I am in agony in these flames." But Abraham said, "Child, remember that during your lifetime you received your good things, and Lazarus in like manner evil things; but now he is comforted here, and you are in agony. Besides all this, between you and us a great chasm has been fixed, so that those who might want to pass from here to you cannot do so, and no one can cross from there to us." He said, "Then, father, I beg you to send him to my father's house - for I have five brothers - that he may warn them, so that they will not also come into this place of torment." Abraham replied, "They have Moses and the prophets; they should listen to them." He said, "No, father Abraham; but if someone goes to them from the dead, they will repent." He said to him, "If they do not listen to Moses and the prophets, neither will they be convinced even if someone rises from the dead."'

Please take a few moments in silence to reflect on the passage, then share a word or phrase that has struck you. Pause to think about what others have said then after a second reading of the passage you may wish to share a further thought.

Reflection

One of the most memorable passages of Scripture is Jesus' healing of the leper (Mark 1:40-45). Pleading on his knees the leper exclaims that Jesus could cure him 'if he wanted to'. Jesus' response was immediate 'of course I want to! Be cured!' Leprosy, we are often told but thankfully rarely if never encounter, is an awful disease. Feeling in the extremities of the body is lost and eyesight often fails. In Jesus' time it meant not simply an illness, which was debilitating and painful, but that the sufferer was shunned and excluded from society. Jesus risked much in talking to the leper, he completely challenged convention in touching him. Like the leper, we are in need of healing; like the leper, we know what Jesus can do for us if we kneel before him and ask (Luke 11:9).

SESSION SIX **LIFT UP YOUR HEARTS**

The parable we have just read provides us with another instance of a man at the margins. Curiously, the poor man in the parable is named – Lazarus; the wealthy man remains anonymous. Whereas in the story of the leper, Jesus' desire was to extend a hand in healing, responding to the need before him, in the parable we see Lazarus, a sick and needy man, being ignored. The story of Jesus makes it clear that the rich man knew Lazarus' name – it wasn't a matter of being unaware of the poverty and illness outside but of ignoring it.

The grand theme for the Jubilee Year of Mercy is 'be merciful as your heavenly Father is merciful' (Luke 6:36). This parable strikes at the very heart of this phrase. We are called by Jesus to demonstrate the mercy that is offered to us by Our Father. The receipt and practice of mercy go hand in hand and, as St John of the Cross so eloquently puts it, 'in the twilight of life, God will not judge us on our earthly possessions and human successes, but on how well we have loved'. Jesus tells this story to demonstrate that our actions, or inactions, will impact us for all eternity! Compassion for Lazarus was possible while both were alive but after death compassion makes no sense and is impossible to demonstrate, it is too late. This parable and that of the unforgiving servant (Matthew 13:21-35; see also MV, 9) give us example not to follow! They warn that providing no room for our ever-Loving Lord can render us immune to his mercy and make us oblivious to opportunities to show mercy. Today has to be the day in which we extend the healing and comfort of Christ to others. Naturally, we remain deeply aware that the plight of others can take a variety of forms – spiritual as well as physical poverty – and the 'poor' can be anyone who needs our attention and whose dignity is offended.

SAINTS OF MERCY: ST KATHERINE DREXEL

Born in 1858, into a prominent and wealthy family, St Katharine was filled with love for God and neighbour. She was primarily concerned with the material and spiritual well-being of black and native Americans. She began by donating money but soon concluded that more people were needed. Katharine founded the Sisters of the Blessed Sacrament for Black and Native American peoples, whose members would work for the betterment of those they were called to serve - at her death more than 500 Sisters were teaching in 63 mission schools.

So, as we dare to say: 'forgive us our trespasses, as we forgive those who trespass against us', we acknowledge the mercy we have been shown, in our contrition and humility, and resolve to joyfully walk his walk (see MV, 15) Like Zacchaeus, like Paul, like so many others through history, a personal encounter with Jesus Christ, the visible face of the invisible, ever-merciful God, causes us to brim over with newness of enthusiasm, compassion and life.

- How much would I say that my Christian faith informs my actions?
- What extra can I resolve to do this year for those in material and spiritual need (see p.62 for the list of corporal and spiritual works of mercy)?
- How might we consider the works of mercy to be acts of justice rather than simply charity?

Closing Prayers – Pope Francis' Prayer for the Year of Mercy (adapted)
You may wish to conclude with the Lord's Prayer, a blessing (p.35 or p.43) or silence.

Lord Jesus Christ,
you have taught us to be merciful like the heavenly Father,
and have told us that whoever sees you sees Him.
Show us your face and we will be saved.

Your loving gaze freed Zacchaeus and Matthew from being enslaved by money;
the adulteress and Magdalene from seeking happiness only in created things;
made Peter weep after his betrayal, and assured Paradise to the repentant thief.

Let us hear, as if addressed to each one of us, the words that you spoke
to the Samaritan woman: "If you knew the gift of God!"

You are the visible face of the invisible Father,
of the God who manifests his power above all by forgiveness and mercy:
let the Church be your visible face in the world, its Lord risen and glorified.

You willed that your ministers would also be clothed in weakness
in order that they may feel compassion for those in ignorance and error:
let everyone who approaches them feel sought after, loved, and forgiven by God.

Send your Spirit and consecrate every one of us with its anointing,
so that the Jubilee of Mercy may be a year of grace from the Lord,
and your Church, with renewed enthusiasm, may bring good news to the poor,
proclaim liberty to captives and the oppressed, and restore sight to the blind.

May your Mother Mary's intercession always avail for us,
you who live and reign with the Father and the Holy Spirit for ever and ever.
Amen.

RESPONDING TO GOD'S MERCY WITH JOY

The spirit of the Lord God is upon me, because the Lord has anointed me; he has sent me to bring good news to the oppressed, to bind up the broken-hearted, to proclaim liberty to the captives, and release to the prisoners; to proclaim the year of the Lord's favour.' (Isaiah 61:1-2).

Re-reading this session's Scripture passage (from the New Revised Standard Version) or perhaps from a different Scripture translation, you may wish to note a word or phrase that caught your attention, here or on your mobile phone, to refer to from time to time.

Holy Scripture is one way which our loving God communicates to each of us. What is your personal response, perhaps an action you might take, to the passage you have just read?

 Empty out the slips of paper from your jam jar and reflect on the goodness, love and mercy that you have experienced and received.

This session explored the intrinsic relationship between faith and a life involved in the service and aid of others. There are many issues in the world today requiring our attention - Jesus exemplifies, he encourages and inspires us to, an integrated life of prayer and compassionate mercy.

SIGNPOST

6. SERVING OTHERS WITH LOVE

My teacher often reads from the Bible to us in class. Some of our favourite stories are the parables like the Good Samaritan and the Lost Son. Sometimes we get read a story that is really hard to understand and the teacher helps us out. The story here, about the rich man and Lazarus, talks about life after death. Out teacher explained that Jesus is using this story to tell the crowd not to ignore those people around us who need help and love.

From the Bible

"There was once a rich man who dressed in the most expensive clothes and lived in great luxury every day. There was also a poor man named Lazarus, covered with sores, who used to be brought to the rich man's door, hoping to eat the bits of food that fell from the rich man's table. The poor man died and was carried by the angels to sit beside Abraham at the feast in heaven. The rich man died and was buried, and in Hades, where he was in great pain, he looked up and saw Abraham, far away, with Lazarus at his side. So he called out, 'Father Abraham! Take pity on me, and send Lazarus to dip his finger in some water and cool off my tongue, because I am in great pain in this fire!' But Abraham said, 'Remember, my son, that in your lifetime you were given all the good things, while Lazarus got all the bad things. But now he is enjoying himself here, while you are in pain. Besides all that, there is a deep pit lying between us, so that those who want to cross over from here to you cannot do so, nor can anyone cross over to us from where you are.'

From the Good News according to St Luke chapter 16 verses 19 to 31.

Can you find the name of the poor man in the story? What about the rich man's name? Have a look at the Bible passage above!

LIFT UP YOUR HEARTS

Jesus tells us in this parable that the very best time we can care for others and help them understand God's message is today. He says that there is no good reason for waiting to help someone if we can. Jesus also promises his support to us. Our job is to try to copy, as well as we can, how Jesus treated others - especially those who everyone else left alone and apart.

Can you find these words in the search box to the right?

Mercy   Love

Service   Life

Charity   Parable

Let us Pray
O God our Father, help me to remember all those who need help and give me and others the strength to do something about it with your Son's help.
Amen.

J	A	Y	X	V	G	L	D	P	E
Y	H	Q	E	C	A	Z	V	R	S
C	W	H	V	S	D	R	J	O	E
R	S	I	O	N	B	U	E	U	R
E	F	C	L	I	F	E	G	F	V
M	D	Q	P	X	T	A	B	K	I
G	H	V	M	Y	R	I	N	Z	C
K	Y	T	I	R	A	H	C	T	E
T	B	L	U	P	W	M	E	F	S
I	C	P	A	R	A	B	L	E	O

DAILY PRAYER
SUNDAY TO SATURDAY

The Office, 'the prayer of the whole People of God' (Pope Paul VI, The Hymn of Praise, 1) is intended to be read communally but here we invite you to use these extracts from the Office as personal daily prayer.

Image: The Crucifixion from the Ulm workshop of Niklaus Weckmann (c.1510)

LIFT UP YOUR HEARTS

SUNDAY - THE LORD LIFTS UP THE LOWLY

Introduction
O God, come to our aid. Lord, make haste to help us.

Glory be to the Father and to the Son and to the Holy Spirit, as it was in the beginning, is now, and ever shall be, world without end. Amen. (Alleluia)
omit Alleluias during Lent

Suggested Hymns
Love divine, all loves excelling
(Celebration for Everyone 398; Laudate 423; Hymns Old & New 337)

Antiphon
This is the time of repentance for us to atone for our sins and seek salvation.

Psalmody   Psalm 112(113)
Praise, O servants of the Lord,
praise the name of the Lord!
May the name of the Lord be blessed
both now and for evermore!
From the rising of the sun to its setting
praised be the name of the Lord!

High above all nations is the Lord,
above the heavens his glory.
Who is like the Lord, our God,
who has risen on high to his throne
yet stoops from the heights to look down,
to look down upon heaven and earth?

From the dust he lifts up the lowly,
from the dungheap he raises the poor
to set them in the company of princes,
yes, with the princes of his people.
To the childless wife he gives a home
and gladdens her heart with children.

Glory be...

Antiphon
This is the time of repentance for us to atone for our sins and seek salvation.

Reading   2 Corinthians 6:1-4
We urge this appeal upon you: you have received the grace of God; do not let it go for nothing. God's own words are: In the hour of my favour I gave heed to you, on the day of deliverance I came to your aid. The hour of favour has now come; now, I say, has the day of deliverance dawned. In order that our service may not be brought into discredit, we avoid giving offence.

Short Responsory
℟ Hear us, Lord, and have mercy, for we have sinned against you.
℣ Listen, Christ, to the prayers of those who cry to you. ℟ Glory be... ℟

Benedictus/Magnificat Antiphon
The Lord is all that I have; the Lord is good to the soul that seeks him.

Benedictus (if said in the morning)
or Magnificat (if said in the evening) -
see inside back cover for these prayers

Pray for the Church, the world and your own personal intercessions
Our Father...

Concluding prayer
Lord, be the beginning and end
of all that we do and say.
Prompt our actions with your grace,
and complete them with your all-powerful help.
Through Christ our Lord.
Amen.

MONDAY - THE LORD IS FULL OF COMPASSION

Introduction
O God, come to our aid. Lord, make haste to help us.

Glory be to the Father and to the Son and to the Holy Spirit, as it was in the beginning, is now, and ever shall be, world without end. Amen. (Alleluia)
omit Alleluias during Lent

Suggested Hymns
O, the love of my Lord
(CFE 570; L 967; HON 430)
O Lord my God, when I in awesome wonder
(CFE 568; L 721; HON 404)

Antiphon
Yours is an everlasting kingdom; Lord your rule lasts from age to age.

Psalmody   Canticle Habakkuk 3:1-19
Lord, I have heard of your fame,
I stand in awe at your deeds.
Do them again in our days and make
   them known.
In spite of your anger, have compassion.

God comes forth from Teman,
the Holy One comes from Mount Paran.
His splendour covers the sky
and his glory fills the earth.
His brilliance is like the light;
rays flash forth from his hands;
there his power lies hidden.

Yet I will rejoice in the Lord
and exult in God my saviour.
The Lord my God is my strength.
He makes me leap like the deer.
He guides me to grace on the heights.

Glory be...

Antiphon
Yours is an everlasting kingdom; Lord your rule lasts from age to age.

Reading   Joel 2:12-13
Come back to me with all your heart, fasting, weeping, mourning. Let your hearts be broken, not your garments torn; turn to the Lord your God again, for he is all tenderness and compassion, slow to anger, rich in graciousness, and ready to relent.

Short Responsory
℟ My sacrifice is a contrite spirit.
℣ A humbled, contrite spirit you will not spurn, O God. ℟ Glory be... ℟

Benedictus/Magnificat Antiphon
Be compassionate as your Father is compassionate, says the Lord.

Benedictus (if said in the morning)
or Magnificat (if said in the evening) -
see inside back cover for these prayers

Pray for the Church, the world and your own personal intercessions
Our Father...

Concluding prayer
Lord God,
you have prepared fitting remedies
   for our weaknesses;
grant that we may reach out gladly
   for your healing grace and
   thereby live in accordance with your will.
We make our prayer through Christ our
   Lord.
Amen.

TUESDAY - THE LORD IS MY HOPE AND SALVATION

Introduction
O God, come to our aid. Lord, make haste to help us.

Glory be to the Father and to the Son and to the Holy Spirit, as it was in the beginning, is now, and ever shall be, world without end. Amen. (Alleluia)

omit Alleluias during Lent

Suggested Hymns
Dear Lord and Father of Mankind
(CFE 143; L 934; HON 116)
Lord, Jesus Christ
(CFE 383; L 772; HON 326)

Antiphon
Lord, heal my soul for I have sinned against you.

Psalmody   Psalm 27(26)
O Lord, hear my voice when I call;
have mercy and answer.
Of you my heart has spoken:
"Seek his face."

It is your face, O Lord, that I seek;
hide not your face.
Dismiss not your servant in anger;
you have been my help.

Do not abandon or forsake me,
O God my help!
Though father and mother forsake me,
the Lord will receive me.

I am sure I shall see the Lord's goodness
in the land of the living.
Hope in him, hold firm and take heart.
Hope in the Lord!

Glory be...

Antiphon
Lord, heal my soul for I have sinned against you.

Reading   2 Thessalonians 2:13-14
But we must always give thanks to God for you, brothers and sisters beloved by the Lord, because God chose you as the first fruits for salvation through sanctification by the Spirit and through belief in the truth. For this purpose he called you through our proclamation of the good news, so that you may obtain the glory of our Lord Jesus Christ.

Short responsory
℟ In the morning let me know your love.
℣ Make me know the way I should walk. ℟
Glory be... ℟

Benedictus/Magnificat Antiphon
Ask, and it will be given to you; seek, and you will find; knock, and the door will be opened to you.

Benedictus (if said in the morning)
or Magnificat (if said in the evening) -
see inside back cover for these prayers

Pray for the Church, the world and your own personal intercessions
Our Father...

Concluding prayer
Lord God,
whose name is holy
and whose mercy is proclaimed in every
  generation:
receive your people's prayer,
and let them sing your greatness with
  never-ending praise.
Amen.

WEDNESDAY - THE LORD GRACES THE HUMBLE

Introduction

O God, come to our aid. Lord, make haste to help us.

Glory be to the Father and to the Son and to the Holy Spirit, as it was in the beginning, is now, and ever shall be, world without end. Amen. (Alleluia)

omit Alleluias during Lent

Suggested Hymns

Amazing Grace
(CFE 40; L 846; HON 36)
Be still and know
(CFE 71; L 909; HON 58)

Antiphon

The Lord is merciful, he gives food to those who fear him to make them remember his wonders.

Psalmody   Psalm 111(110)

I will thank the Lord with all my heart
in the meeting of the just and their assembly.
Great are the works of the Lord,
to be pondered by all who love them.

Majestic and glorious his work,
his justice stands firm for ever.
He makes us remember his wonders.
The Lord is compassion and love.

He gives food to those who fear him;
keeps his covenant ever in mind.
He has shown his might to his people
by giving them the lands of the nations.

His works are justice and truth,
his precepts are all of them sure,
standing firm for ever and ever;
they are made in uprightness and truth.

Glory be...

Antiphon

The Lord is merciful, he gives food to those who fear him to make them remember his wonders.

Reading   1 Peter 5:5-7

Clothe yourselves with humility in your dealings with one another, for
'God opposes the proud, but gives grace to the humble.'
Humble yourselves therefore under the mighty hand of God, so that he may exalt you in due time. Cast all your anxiety on him, because he cares for you.

Short responsory

℟ I said: 'Lord, have mercy on me.'
℣ 'Heal my soul for I have sinned against you.' ℟ Glory be... ℟

Benedictus/Magnificat Antiphon

My soul magnifies the Lord, since God has had regard for my humble state.

Benedictus (if said in the morning)
or Magnificat (if said in the evening) -
see inside back cover for these prayers

Pray for the Church, the world and your own personal intercessions
Our Father...

Concluding prayer

Lord God,
you crown the merits of the saints
and pardon sinners when they repent.
Forgive us our sins, now that we come before you,
humbly confessing our guilt.
Through Christ our Lord.
Amen.

LIFT UP YOUR HEARTS

THURSDAY - THE LORD'S ONLY BEGOTTEN SON

Introduction
O God, come to our aid. Lord, make haste to help us.

Glory be to the Father and to the Son and to the Holy Spirit, as it was in the beginning, is now, and ever shall be, world without end. Amen. (Alleluia)

omit Alleluias during Lent

Suggested Hymns
Lord Jesus, think on me
(CFE 384; L 204; HON 327)
God forgave my sin in Jesus' name
(CFE 209; L 849; HON 175)

Antiphon
Christ the Lord was tempted and suffered for us. Come, let is adore him.

Psalmody   Psalm 92(91)

It is good to give thanks to the Lord,
to make music to your name, O Most High,
to proclaim your love in the morning
and your truth in the watches of the night

Your deeds, O Lord, have made me glad;
for the work of your hands I shout with joy.

O Lord, how great are your works!
How deep are your designs!

To me you give the wild ox's strength;
you anoint me with the purest oil.
The just will flourish like the palm tree
and grow like a Lebanon cedar.

Planted in the house of the Lord
they will flourish in the courts of our God,
to proclaim that the Lord is just.
In him, my rock, there is no wrong.

Glory be...

Antiphon
Christ the Lord was tempted and suffered for us. Come, let is adore him.

Reading   Isaiah 53:4-5
Ours were the sufferings he bore, ours the sorrows he carried. But we, we thought of him as someone punished, struck by God, and brought low. He was pierced through for our faults, crushed for our sins. On him lies a punishment that brings peace, and through his wounds we are healed.

Short Responsory
℟ A pure heart create for me, O God.
℣ Put a steadfast spirit within me. ℟
Glory be... ℟

Benedictus/Magnificat Antiphon
I have done many good works for you to see, says the Lord; for which of these good works do you wish to kill me?

Benedictus (if said in the morning)
or Magnificat (if said in the evening) –
see inside back cover for these prayers

Pray for the Church, the world and your own personal intercessions
Our Father...

Concluding prayer
Lord God,
whose surpassing mercy blessed us with the unfathomable riches of Christ,
grant that we may grow in knowledge
   of you,
yield fruit in every good work,
and by the truth of the Gospel
live faithfully in your presence.
Through Christ our Lord. Amen.

FRIDAY - THE LORD'S WILL BE DONE

Introduction
O God, come to our aid. Lord, make haste
to help us.

Glory be to the Father and to the Son
and to the Holy Spirit, as it was in the
beginning, is now, and ever shall be, world
without end. Amen. (Alleluia)

omit Alleluias during Lent

Suggested Hymns
Make me a channel of your peace
(CFE 478; L 898; HON 342)
Father I place into your hands
(CFE 159; L 971; HON 133)

Antiphon
Anyone who follows me will not be walking
in the dark; he will have the light of life.

Psalmody   Psalm 145(144)
I will give you glory, O God my king,
I will bless your name for ever.
The Lord is great, highly to be praised,
his greatness cannot be measured.

Age to age shall proclaim your works,
shall declare your mighty deeds,
shall speak of your splendour and glory,
tell the tale of your wonderful works.

The Lord is kind and full of compassion,
slow to anger, abounding in love.
How good is the Lord to all,
compassionate to all his creatures.

Glory be...

Antiphon
Anyone who follows me will not be walking
in the dark; he will have the light of life.

Reading   Romans 12:1-2
I implore you by God's mercy to offer
your very selves to him: a living sacrifice,
dedicated and fit for his acceptance, the
worship offered by mind and heart. Adapt
yourselves no longer to the pattern of
this present world, but let your minds
be remade and your whole nature thus
transformed. Then you will be able to
discern the will of God, and to know what
is good, acceptable and perfect.

Short Responsory
℟ From my sins turn away your face.
℣ And blot out my guilt. ℟ Glory be... ℟

Benedictus/Magnificat Antiphon
Whoever does the will of my Father, says the
Lord, is my brother, my sister, and mother.

Benedictus (if said in the morning)
or Magnificat (if said in the evening) -
see inside back cover for these prayers

Pray for the Church, the world and your
own personal intercessions
Our Father...

Concluding prayer
Almighty, ever-living God,
it is your will to unite the entire universe
under your beloved Son,
Jesus Christ, the King of heaven and earth.
Grant freedom to the whole of creation,
and let it praise and serve your majesty
for ever.
Through Christ our Lord.
Amen.

LIFT UP YOUR HEARTS

SATURDAY - THE LORD RESCUES US FROM DARKNESS

Introduction

O God, come to our aid. Lord, make haste to help us.

Glory be to the Father and to the son and to the Holy Spirit, as it was in the beginning, is now, and ever shall be, world without end. Amen. (Alleluia)

omit Alleluias during Lent

Suggested Hymns

Christ be our light
(CFE 891; L 883)
Lead us, heavenly Father
(CFE 351; L 315; HON 298)

Antiphon

Anyone who follows me will not be walking in the dark; he will have the light of life.

Psalmody   Psalm 51(50)

Have mercy on me, God, in your kindness.
In your compassion blot out my offence.
O wash me more and more from my guilt
and cleanse me from my sin.

My offences truly I know them;
my sin is always before me
Against you, you alone, have I sinned;
what is evil in your sight I have done.

Indeed you love truth in the heart;
then in the secret of my heart teach me
   wisdom.
O purify me, then I shall be clean;
O wash me, I shall be whiter than snow.

Make me hear rejoicing and gladness,
that the bones you have crushed may revive. From my sins turn away your face and blot out all my guilt.

Glory be...

Antiphon

Anyone who follows me will not be walking in the dark; he will have the light of life.

Reading   Colossians 1:12-13

Give thanks, with joy, to the Father, who has made you fit to have a share of what God has reserved for his people in the kingdom of light. He has rescued us from the power of darkness and brought us safe into the kingdom of his dear Son.

Short Responsory

℟ Your word, O Lord, will endure for ever.
℣ Your truth will last from age to age. ℟
Glory be... ℟

Benedictus/Magnificat Antiphon

The tax collector stood afar off and did not dare to raise his eyes to heaven. He beat his breast and said, 'God, be merciful to me, a sinner.'

Benedictus (if said in the morning)
or Magnificat (if said in the evening) -
see inside back cover for these prayers

Pray for the Church, the world and your own personal intercessions
Our Father...

Concluding prayer

Lord,
break the bonds of sin
which our weaknesses have forged to
   enchain us,
and in your loving mercy forgive your
   people's guilt.
We make our prayer through Christ our
   Lord.
Amen.

THE WORKS OF MERCY

'In the twilight of life, God will not judge us on our earthly possessions and human successes, but on how well we have loved' (St John of the Cross).

Where our brothers and sisters have been hungry and thirsty, in need of comfort and affection, we shall be judged on our response. Equally, hunger and thirst can relate to the spiritual – we are, after all, not only physical beings but are both body and soul (cf. CCC, 2447). To this end, here are the fourteen works of mercy listed, as pairs, for your reflection (for reference the Scriptural references are included). The Spiritual works are listed in green.

On the opposite page feel free to make notes how you, your group or your parish already undertake the 14 works and how you might extend their practice.

Feed the Hungry (Matthew 25:35)
Instruct the Ignorant (1 Ezra 7:25) Feeding the body and also the mind & soul

Give Drink to the Thirsty (Matthew 25:35)
Counsel the Doubtful (Daniel 4:1-24) We also thirst for truth and righteousness

Clothe the Naked (Matthew 25:36)
Admonish the Sinner (Proverbs 28:23) Exposed through sin, denuded of grace, we are to practise and preach repentance

Shelter the Homeless (Matthew 25:35)
Bear Wrongs Patiently (Hebrews 12:1-4) Carry our daily cross as Jesus did to shelter humanity

Visit the Sick (Matthew 25:36)
Forgive all Injuries (Matthew 6:12; 28:21-22) Healing through forgiveness and mercy, both for ourselves and for those we forgive

Visit the Imprisoned (Matthew 25:36)
Comfort the Sorrowful (John 21:19-38) Helping those imprisoned in sorrow, loneliness and depression

Bury the Dead (Tobit 4:3-8)
Pray for the Living (James 5:16)
and the Dead (2 Maccabees 12:38-46) Prayer and action together for those gone before us marked with the sign of faith

---

LIFT UP YOUR HEARTS

Image: The Seven Works of Mercy (Corporal) by Frans Francken the Younger (1605)

HOW CAN I MAKE THIS A REALITY?

Some other booklets in the exploring faith group sharing series

Love Divine (published autumn 2015)
Six group sessions for faith-sharing which explore the grace we receive in the sacraments of the Church and how we are called to respond.

978-0-9927584-5-5   £2.00 where sold

Amazing Grace (published Lent 2013)
Six group sessions for faith-sharing exploring the call to continuing conversion and the mercy and love shown by God to his children.

978-0-9570793-6-6   £1.50 where sold

Jesus, My Lord (published autumn 2014)
Six group sessions for faith-sharing which explore the call of every Christian to an ever closer discipleship with our Lord, Jesus Christ.

978-0-9927584-1-7   £2.00 where sold

Anointed! (published Lent 2015)
Six group sessions for faith-sharing which explore, our sharing in Jesus Christ's life and mission as priest, prophet and king.

978-0-9927584-4-8   £2.00 where sold

Previous resources in the exploring faith series can be viewed on the Diocese of Westminster's website. Further copies of this booklet and other resources may be bought from **www.houseonrock.co.uk**. If you have a QR reader simply scan the code (right) and you will be directed to the relevant webpage or call 01227 362669.

---

exploring faith booklets are produced, under licence, by **houseonrock.co.uk**

LIFT UP YOUR HEARTS